CAUC/ASIAN

Dearest Vanessa,
Thanks for all your
support & friendship.
Hope you enjoy,

Neethe /x

First published in 2023 by Blue Diode Press
30 Lochend Road
Leith
Edinburgh EH6 8BS
www.bluediode.co.uk

ISBN: 978-1-915108-11-1

Typesetting: Rob A. Mackenzie. text in Minion Pro

Cover art: Amber Kunaratnam
Cover design and typography: Rob A. Mackenzie and Fran Hodgson

Diode logo design: Sam and Ian Alexander.

Printed and bound by Imprint Digital, Exeter, UK.
https://digital.imprint.co.uk

CAUC/ASIAN

Neetha Kunaratnam

BLUE DIODE PRESS

to my girls, with love

Contents

Home

June 23, 2016

I

Go Home. We voted leave...
Her jaw trembled
as she seethed,

and the deadpan response
I might have mustered
froze on my lips,

as she brandished
a crumpled flyer
and unleashed its litany of stats.

I'm going I said
and melted away,
too saddened to understand

how the idea
of nation thrives on
intransigent borders,

how our identities were hijacked
by a binary ballot
endorsed by the bluster of bigots.

II

Home is a sanctuary where
my daughter decants
a kaleidoscope of watercolors
onto her honeyed skin,

and we smile at our favorite animation,
as a lion communes with all the animals
in a stop-motion multicultural vision.

Home is the kitchen where we concoct fusions
with spices we've blended by hand
in an heirloom pestle and mortar.

And *home* is my mother in whom for years
I was landlocked,
when she was my country and compass,

and all I knew was hunger and impulse,
and territory was a concept pinned to a wall
like a patchwork atlas made of felt.

III

In this England of unkindness
sanctioned by suits waxing impolitic
their xenophobic bleats,

I heard that a pregnant friend,
betraying her German lilt,
was told to repatriate

by a man close to death,
as she consoled her feverish child
in the doctor's waiting room.

IV

And I want to say home is where the heart is, and ask those who
   would banish us
to grip my arteries with sullen fists, and pull the sinews taut like
   guy ropes
so I can camp out under my heart's stretched skin, and be
   nomadic wherever
they want to shunt me.

V

Consider…

When last I flew home, to the island my father had quit
before it spliced into tribes,

I sought to subvert the exile my parents had imposed
for fear of persecution and petrol bombs.

I imagined my heritage could be a badge woven
from snippets of a phrasebook,

as I journeyed home in the days
after the armistice had been brokered

to see, in twenty years away,
that the country had been broken,

and I was stranded
like a tourist clutching his Lonely Planet.

Go Home? Or did you
mean *get lost?*

Seed

'Say that the leaves are harvested when
they have rotted into the mold. Call that
profit.' —WENDELL BERRY

The man who sought the patent
heard the court decree
that he alone had fathered the Seed.

Accorded sole custody,
he was deemed the proprietor
of a potent new variety,

which he rented to growers
hooked on bumper yields,
and blind to the small print.

The gathering wind
caused the tampered Seed
to trespass into adjacent fields,

where an aggrieved farmer,
sweating in the maize,
was led to believe

that swathes of her grain
had been colonised
by loyal company men,

whose manicured hands
held demands to pursue
every single breach of copyright.

Raising a callused palm,
the farmer bid them retreat,
then stole inside to bubble-wrap

her seasoned archive of
patiently dried seeds,
which she posted to friends,

having refused the contract
her neighbour had signed,
in which he'd agreed not to

stockpile, store, save, freeze,
pocket, replant, swap, cross-breed,
appropriate, lose, mislay, steal,

mishandle, loan or abscond with
the Seed, nor allow it
to cluster under his nails.

Unearthed

1/

Trees conceived as commodity,
as firewood chopped to slake
relentless demand. In starlit bivouacs,
loggers ached in their bones.

Roots were snapped like necks until
the forest bled out and flatlined.
And indignation subsumed
the indigenous heart like a lock.

2/

Years passed. Speculators scoured flatlands
with blundering machines, extracting
fossils, and excavating flames,
convinced that God had granted them

a monopoly on sacred water;
to resurrect carbon compressed
in smashed shale, and scarred sand,
and the bones of decayed birds.

3/

Black blood chemically thinned
thunders down the steel aorta,
like a snake thrusting past farms,
to hiss at the river's blockade.

There the custodians of Standing Rock
have defied snowdrift and red tape,
as their battered bodies resist
the transgressions of *zuzeca sape*.

A bruised veteran performs
prostrations on the road. I can't
believe he doesn't flinch, as the sun
melts tar into the sebum of his hair.

An Eco-Worrier Tweets

#inappropriate
to appropriate fossils,
as contract drillers
toy with tectonics
to exhume the trapped sun.

#object
to objectives that the market knows,
the objectification of
leaf as price tag,
of bark as barcode.

#resist
supply aka monopoly,
demand à la ransom.
Supplant the tyranny
of the engineered seed.

#inventorise
as they make ash of ash,
while we pine for the pines,
and they plane the mighty planes
and box the boxes into lines.

#denounce
these apparatchiks of plastic
who want it now, who want it quick,
as fat cats sing of apocalypse
from puckered lips.

Cauc/asian

Rush hour. Racing the clock.
Headed to the bowling lanes
for the Brownies trip,
then on to mail the PCR
before last post,

but must first heed
the warning light
to stop for gas,
placate my daughter
who's stressed
we're gonna be late.

Step out. Unscrew the cap
in the warm evening
haze of the tiny forecourt.
Urge the unleaded
to the brim, as a white
minivan pulls up,
three young Caucasians,
all six packs and drill.

Driver calls out
excuse me? three times,
and time doesn't slow
to help decide if
I can squeeze in this chat,

or file his exhortation under
Sorry, can't stop or
How might I help? rather than
the guilty sub-plot of
Why hast thou forsaken me?

Choosing Good Samaritan,
I glance up to see his grin.
                    Know what you need?
Oh. A troll, all alpha
and sing-song sneer,
a veneer of smarm
in the challenge, bolshy
and grating.

Try to backtrack, revert to blank,
ghost him, but he insists
on rasping the punchline
with relish –
                    More revs, mate!

A combustible leer.
Can't retreat from this farce,
so cast him a withering look.
                    Oh, someone's in a mood
he jests, feigning bonhomie.

Attempt reason then.
No, I'm not. Just in a rush.
Daughter's in the car. For real.
Appreciate if you'd back off.

On high alert, worried
what my daughter will think,
how to explain that some people are
in it for kicks to the gut.
Focus back on the throb and glug
of petrol, the whir of the pump.
Come on. It's almost topped up.

My peripheral vision senses his
retreat, vexed perhaps from
concluding there's no need

to ridicule this older man
in front of his kin.

His door slams.
And as I watch him
pull away, our eyes
lock into a death stare
whose intensity hurts,
the thought seeping in
that maybe my skin had
attracted his bile.

Innocuous, yet glaring:
middle-class, middle-aged,
salt and pepper, Asian.

Which vindictiveness I'll suspect
but never prove, able only
to bear witness to
the daggers when
his malice was spurned –

tyres squealing, rubber
tattooing the tarmac,
his eyeballs agog,
as the primal roar
comes full circle –
                    More Revs! See, told ya!

Equally fuelled by testosterone,
there I am still, ambushed
by the ego, hot cheeked and
bemused to the point
of aggression, my two fingers
flailing in the air
like a slumped erection.

Frackers

«Il est trop tard pour être pessimiste.»
—YANN-ARTHUS BERTRAND

Wrackers churn up the clay, smash fossils with chemical sprays
      until the frail shale frays then cracks.
Trackers confirm in pristine data
      that no toxins have spilled in the aquifers of our gut.
      No febrile fish, no moulting birds, no barren cows, declare the
Frackers who've spun these landscapes
      as fractals on infinite maps.

Wreckers force-feed the land their hydraulic deluge
      of carcinogens and sand.
Trekkers with deep voiceovers
      praise entrepreneurs *who've gone*
      where no man has gone before, and
Freckers as feckless as water cannons,
      indulge themselves in seismic abandon.

Wrickers fuel rickety debate,
      wittering their reasons in haste.
Trickers dictate demand, spark supply,
      and trickle-down myths about
      doomed eco-lifestyles. And all the while
Frickers flaunt their economic fripperies,
        to freak out the twitterati
        posting fricative soliloquies.

Wrockers drill granite, incubate through pipelines, as truculent
Trockers project profits in quadrillions,
      and TV showcases dextrous
Frockers, dressed in consequentialist tropes
      of high yield, who strut in hard hats and suits
        on tightropes strung far
        above the moral high ground.

Wruckers wreak a ruckus
        in the boardroom brawl,
        as the market projects mid-term mirth;
Truckers pump lakeloads of slurry
        through quintuplex tubing
        into the unsuspecting earth;
Fruckers cause a fracas
        as they step on the gas, OD on cash,
        and siphon off the last reserves
        at the ticker tape jamboree.

Messages in plastic bottles

To finders, for keeps

1/

Pounded by the sea's fists –
cutlery cracked in transit,
polythene-sheathed lego bricks,
yoghurt tubs destined to drift.

2/

Tupperware, draped in kelp, trails onto shore, zombie-like.
A straw, piercing a turtle's nostril, incubates a saline death.

3/

Lured by algae's sulphurous whiff, gulls swoop for krill
on cubes of mottled plastic
that stuck in their gullets, kill.

4/

Six pack rings collar seals and garrotte their cubs.
Barbie doll shards stab jellyfish, dislocated limbs bob.

5/

Bottle tops transform oil spills into mosaics.
Tarpaulin makes a piecemeal shroud for dying coral reefs.

6/

Fleeces unravel their microfibres. Plankton feed
on these synthetic délices. Plastic motes enter the tracts of
famished fish.

7/

The ocean's a laminated mosaic, polystyrene icebergs
flaunting indestructible polymers.

8/

The waves' origami coughs up blow-up dolls like withered skins.
Milk cartons, surfing plastic limbo, seek Tetrapak heaven.

Private

As I quit this lawned campus
where education is private,
two Apaches thunder past,
drilling the sky with decibels.

And I drive home in a harried sweat,
past these hoardings that mask
the facelift of a boarding house,
where study is secondary.

Wondering where their hellfire
might land, I consider how
a father shields his daughters
with a carapace of molten flesh;

how he's racked by guilt,
because his girls never asked
for factories to fashion numbers
into dust and numbness.

And as the drone subsides,
I'm ashamed of my complicity,
my salary that subsidises missiles
that subdivide casualties.

So I pray for the privacy
of those who convalesce *in camera,*
jagged windows boarded up
to dissuade all but the saviours.

Planet Earth

1/

Oblivious to her voyeurs,
Nature describes her slick metamorphoses
                              in a thousand fast-tracked sequences.
Seedlings surge, leaves curve,
                    the calyx glows and sepals unfurl,
                              petals unclasp and stamens extend.

2/

And I confess that these fuchsias, locked in a playback loop,
seem to bloom in perpetuity,
          which suggests that we, or they, resist the narrative of decay.

3/

And to watch time hotfoot its chronology, to meld through
the montage of transitions
                              as autumn hurtles into winter –
and leaves shrivel, and ice flecks onto bare larch –
is somehow to claim mastery
over the momentum of the seasons
because a thumb can pause snow, and rewind death itself.

4/

Pan to a soundtrack of strings as
                    hermit crabs shack up in mannequin heads
crows flee the *airpocalypse* of toxic smog,
                    ants make exodus from trampled mud,
a glut of chickadees cough up yarrow seed and blood.

5/

The documentary of epiphanies
makes us feel omniscient
as if
we can backtrack on disaster
as if
tabula rasa is an airbrushed landscape.

El Dorado

The mechanised arcs of constant sprinklers
spurt a carbaryl rain, and its fine spray
beefs up the grapes in the parched soil.
Drip lines palliate the sirocco dust.

On the driest days, in the vineyards
that still trust hands over machines,
the grape pickers uncurl velcro tongues,
but resist the urge to sip from the sky.

Protected in long sleeves, they towel down
and hydrate from bidons, kneeling
to pluck the firmest Merlot, for which
the aquifers have been sucked dry.

The Mirror

The birdie's fighting itself!
they cry, as you rush out,
both kids all eyes and awe

as the starling defends
its patch from the doppelgänger
that's ghosted into sight.

Its beak hammers
cracks into the glass like
an appalling metronome,

as you shepherd the kids inside,
to shield them from
this suicide by reflection.

Sunlight stuns the aggressor
into a dazed sort of cognition,
as you snatch away its adversary.

Restoring to its kingdom
the logic of footprint, scent
and song, you lean the old mirror

against the kitchen wall, beneath
its spotless successor. Outside,
the speckled bird shakes a worm free.

Cat Concerto

Dapper in his tux, Tom enters stage left,
traipsing, chin up, towards the Steinway.
Bowing haughtily, coat tails swishing,

this virtuoso cat fishes out a hanky
to dry his deft fingers, though
they're sheathed in silk gloves.

He smooths his lapels, pausing for effect,
then caresses the keys, before tenderly
edging his digits into a rhapsody

which stirs the dormant mouse,
who's nestled in the hammers
of the piano's domino mechanism.

Jerry's jarred awake, a murine pinball
gathering momentum until he lands,
bum first, on a tightrope of strings.

He wants to restore his pillowed peace,
and punish this feline maestro –
this bow tied architect of

his shattered dreamscape – so up
he jumps to wag his finger at Tom
with a mock conductor's flourish.

The logic of revenge also dictates
he upstage the cat in an act
of public sabotage, and as Jerry

covets an Oscar for slapstick,
he slams down the lid, turning
Tom's paws into convulsing spiders,

then snips at his balletic fingers with
scissors synchronised to spill no
blood, before laying on the ivories

a gleaming mousetrap that
threatens Tom's dextrous digits
with a bouquet of bruises.

Tom responds with increased rubato,
the hammers oscillating as if
Jerry's astride a bucking bronco.

And it's tit for tat as mouse and cat
wrestle for tempo, for the right to
jazz it up and defer the crescendo…

…by which time, they're both wrecks,
Tom's sleeves fallen, his cummerbund
unravelled, his forehead kissing the keys,

as Jerry milks the canned applause in
a DJ designed to towel off sweat,
and hide his cuts and bruises.

And as the velvet curtain falls,
the eager children replay the clip,
hoping Tom will win the next round,

and the contest go to sudden death.

Tragi-comic

The Gold Rush, 1925

Charlie's boiled the boot like a turkey
with the panache of a snowbound gourmet
to salute those who ate their shoes to survive,

and Mack glares at the basting water
Charlie's spooning over the serving dish after
he's boiled the boot like a turkey.

Mack plays the scene for laughs,
reluctantly chews the liquorice like it's leather
to salute those who ate their shoes to survive.

Charlie picks the hobnails clean of gristle,
and fork-twists the spaghetti laces to make-believe
he's boiled the boot like a turkey.

The cutting room floor is a flood of film stock,
and Charlie and Mack snooze, spent from trying
to salute those who ate their shoes to survive.

For they hadn't imagined the stomach cramps,
or the laxative effects of their obsessive mimesis
when Charlie boiled the boot like a turkey
to salute those who ate their shoes to survive.

Trolley Problems

1/

Whether to scour the wheelie bins / or stockpile the bargains
in my hunter-gatherer's trolley,
then jettison half the spoils /
or let it trundle, overladen / away from me.

2/

Whether to privilege innocence / or utility,
        steer into five static kids / or piñata one plucky VIP,
        employ magical realism / or allegory,
        transcribe the gory detail / or refer you to a footnote
                on Trolleyology.

3/

Whether to admit to *hit and run* / or tamper with the CCTV,
skid on spilt milk / or avoid the clean-up on aisle three,
freewheel out of this superstore / or linger listlessly.

4/

Whether to acquire self-drive technology:

preserve my moral agency / or lament its lobotomy,
upgrade to front suspension / or ten-inch alloy wheels,
rebrand myself as gin seller / or sometime mobile library.

5/

Whether to cash in my franchise / or pursue abstract quandaries
to buy shares in weapons / or kindness in equities,
to play footsie with the markets / or build a wall on Wall Street.

6/

Whether to court the journals of an intellectual elite /
or refine my torchlit-spray-can-technique,

to number my dilemmas / or bullet point my grief,
to pander to philosophy / or philander with poetry,

to ditch for good the either / or dichotomy.

Brexit means Breakfast

Sourced from local ingredients, where possible

Wurst case scenario
Britwurst, blockwurst, tikka masala wurst

Selection of pains
In the neck, in the arse
O, no raisins
O confectionery
Perdu, aka non-French stick

Eggstravaganza
Nightingale (ex Florentine)
Benny Hill (ex Benedict)
Soft boiled with HM soldiers
Scotch and quail

Wondrous wheat fields
Assortment of tempting cereals

Faraged from the hedgerow
Selection of scotberries, taffberries, pomberries, celtberries
And their jams and jellies

A choice of coffees
Liverpudlian latte, Mancunian macchiato,
Midlothian mocha, Cheshire cappuccino

Rotten Fruit and Veg

Having lost its cool, a cucumber is on the rampage with a handheld blender. Peas are being advised to observe curfew and avoid the city centre.

There was indecent exposure in Cincinnati as peaches mooned at nectarines, who retaliated by turning the other cheek.

A pumpkin has had its licence revoked for reckless speeding around midnight on Disney Boulevard.

Radicalised rhubarb are being remanded in custody for inciting hate crime against buckwheat.

Oranges are today suing clementines for copyright infringement. Mandarins and tangerines are set to appeal.

In Greenwich Village, Jazz apples have been accused of excessive scat, and other instances of non-PC backchat.

Charges of identity fraud have been upheld in the cases of banana aka long yellowberry, blackberry aka indigo drupe, and pear aka speckled pome.

A broccoli boiled within an inch of its life is in critical condition. Fruitarians have condemned this as an act of aggression.

A Merlot has been indicted for raisin' hell in Yolo County, California. A grapefruit, previously under suspicion, has been acquitted and pardoned.

Banana republicans are lobbying to increase freshwater tax in new legislation that has been widely condemned as daylight raspberry.

In Santiago, Chile, a jalapeño and a scotch bonnet have plead guilty to arson.

Having crossbred avocados and pomegranates, scientists have crashed the market with counterfeit rubies.

(dead white men)

Who commodified the body, and ratified its currency,
ditching slavery when the profits stymied.
Who preached autonomy for the *noblesse* only,
with clean-ups and climbdowns rife in the colonies.

Who cautioned their daughters about eugenics,
but still desired the exotic, who sired secret bastards away
from sorry spouses, shunned the swarthy
progeny, and spurned the surrogate mothers.

Who drew borders with rulers, straight and crooked.
Who aspired to be sun-kissed but perplexed, turned grey.
Who morphed into matriarchs, squirming in bodices,
like mistresses of phallic philosophies.

Who've evolved into lords with jaundiced tans,
who covet silver spoons and bleach their teeth.
Who sip at cocktails, demanding punctual sunsets
and bucolic vistas cleansed of refugee tents.

Who delegate nurture to nannies, presence to pacifiers,
day-care to dummies, and sell their sperm for cash.
Whose henchmen serve as caddies,
manicuring lawns, muzzle-bound, smiles still intact.

Who lounge in the crisis of the overheating sun,
as sprinklers kiss their grass iridescent.
Who nuke the bindweed's white flower trumpets,
as their tired, old tongues are devoured by wasps.

Who wind up the crowd until it heaves and breaks.
Who bristle in their graves, denouncing snowflakes.

Duck three ways

1/ Foie gras

Connoisseurs plump
for terrines
steeped in
armagnac jus,
scoff at
tinned *foie gras*
for the masses,
blaming the EU

for cultural fusions
which dilute
this svelte mousse
so it's served
with paprika
in Budapest,
or sold to America
with fries.

And the parliament
-arians of the elite
gorge on all
the accoutrements –
fig, pickled pear,
truffle shavings.

2/ Gavage

Aka
birds bulge
in lawful tradition,
aka

state-protected,
force-fed,
liver-fattening,
aka
plastic pipe
pushed past beak
1 metre
down throat,
aka
farmer grips bird
by neck,
palm flattened
on squirming back,
aka
pneumatic pump
shunts down
fat-boiled corn
from big
yellow funnel.

3/ *Finition d'engraissement*

according to bureaucrats it's
the standardised swelling
of the bird
performed like clockwork
three times per day
for three weeks,

according to factory tourists
it's a bird-centric season of
Punch and Judy,
a *commedia dell'arte*
of balloon sculpture,
meant to enlarge a liver
to ten times its size.

Quality checks
are indexed
according to
the liver's proportion
of blood-filled veins –
A ends up in pâtés,
B flash fried,
C in sauces or
bulk buys online.

Freight

1/

Thirty-nine Vietnamese migrants,
fragile freight, frozen in a lorry
in Essex. Their fatal embarkment
brokered just days before by
middlemen on a twilit border.

2/

Thirty-nine nomads trafficked
at a premium, no refund
guaranteed. The contraband
body made tender.

3/

Faraway families
unable to bear witness
to the misgivings
of their children
as they stow away
like precious cargo in
the dark deprivation of
the refrigeration trailer.

4/

No common language
for the passengers to convey
doubt to the driver fixed
on his destination,
driven to distraction
by the lure of cash on delivery.

5/

SMS like epitaphs that
triangulate the times of their death.
Forensics chart the data
of their thirty-nine failed hearts,
scouring the hyperthermic coffin,
as fraught kin plead
to embassies to fund
the corpses' return.

6/

And newsfeeds cling
tight to the numbers
as words fail to
approximate the pain.

Vigilant/e

In which the young heir to
an industrialist's empire
is beset by tunnel vision —
pearls trickling like gunshots
down the dark spine of an alley;
his parents unexpectedly slain
in a first world allegory
that transcends its station,
as if vengeance is an urge
common to all humanity.
In which teenage therapy with
an overpriced shrink helps him
manage his anger; and in
guided shamanic visions,
he's reborn as a bat —
insomniac, alert, fretful.

Countless spin-offs spawn
across pale patriarchies,
in which only the strain
of his masochism varies.
A scholarly version surfaces,
in which his brooding begets
rumination so intense that
he will major in phenomenology,
devour *What It's Like To Be a Bat*,
question his assumed identity.
Rejecting conceit, and bad faith,
he dispenses with kevlar, and
the hand-stitched amnesia
of the enveloping cape.

There's a Zen parable in which
he relives his parents' demise
through *their* eyes, first numbness,
then release — until he steadily
unshackles from the suffering.
Adopting the bat as a symbol of
reincarnation, he ordains in
monastic life. Nurtures unhurried
compassion over decades of
devotion. Uncouples pain from
torment. Called home to bury
his butler, he's unfazed by the loss,
anchored in its rituals. *Vigilant.*

After the wake, subsumed by the city,
he stumbles too soon upon a felony.
Nearing the scene, he eyes
the aggressor with a mirror's
limpid clarity. And in slo-mo
montage reflects all ill intent
back on the youth, who weeps,
repents, beseeches clemency.
Onlookers are disarmed by
such nonchalant non-violence.

And the dharma hero
in his coffee-coloured cowl
vows henceforth to levy
such transformation in
as many souls as his
remaining days will allow.
Redemption without bloodshed.
In which I see a helluva story,
but accept its lack of
box office appeal.

#45 interrupts this poem to mansplain his supremacist legacy

(If words wound and acronyms axe...)

*National 'I Got Guns' Association/ Nepotism Is God's Gift Always/
News Indicts Good Government Acts/ NB I Groped Gusset Avidly/
Naked I Grasped Gasoline Arses/ Nearly Impeached Glum Glam
Addicts/ Nationalism Is Goddam Gangsta Awesome/ Nazi Illusions
Gather Grim Assassins/ Navajo, Iroquois, Genuflecting German
Aryans/ Negative Interference Gets Grand Applause/ Number
Ignorance Garners Gleeful Acclaim/ Nihilism Intimidates Green
Greta Army/ Nuke Illogical Girl Gone AWOL/ Nevertheless I Grin
Glittering Air/ Neutered Intellects Grapple Grim Arithmetic/ Nasty
Intimidation Gets Good Appeal/ Nothing I Grow Gives Affection/
Now I Greedily Grab Adulation/ Nobody Is Getting Great,
America/ Nowhere Is Gonna Glitter Again/ Not If Germs Gravely
Assemble*

(... How can silence soothe?)

Cities of the Nation

i.m. GF

Praise saga-city in this crude conster-nation
Denounce fero-city in the cruel imagi-nation

Cheer the simpli-city of utopian expla-nation
Resist the toxi-city of hot indig-nation

Charge with electri-city against elimi-nation
Fear rapa-city in the sick condem-nation

Hail perspica-city in the fog of stag-nation
Lament incapa-city in the flawed abomi-nation

Marvel at auda-city in the bright fasci-nation
Unpick the opa-city of the chauvinist's determi-nation

Salvage vera-city in the scorched desti-nation
Fight compli-city in the blind discrimi-nation

Combat the infeli-city of crass subordi-nation
Sigh for the menda-city in his renomi-nation

Let love trump dupli-city in full deto-nation
and group with tena-city in the pale alie-nation

Lo the burning cities across the denomi-nation
and the ethni-city of angels, here in dam-nation

Between the Buddha and the Batman

Between the Buddha and the Batman,
vigil and vigilante,
oxytocin or adrenaline for the rage.

Between science and suggestion,
technicians scrutinise toxins,
pinpoint therapies for the pain.

Between the Buddha and the Batman,
between periphery and brink,
we're sleepwalking in Angerland.

Between armistice and ahisma,
creased treaties hatch into peace cranes,
their wings flecked heavy with ink.

Between the Buddha and the Batman,
lotus posture and clenched fist,
mercenaries thrive on the collateral.

Between the fanboys and studio execs,
multiplexes churn out
an excess of popcorn shrapnel.

Between the Buddha and the Batman,
some pray for poppies to stopper pistols,
and poems to be penned from their petals.

Between the vows and the vengeance
there's a pacifist hanging limp
from a noose of daisy chains.

Between the Buddha and the Batman,
poised between faith and fury,
banyan tree and belfry break in my brain.

Quarantine

1/

isolate from yourself to find a void.
embrace its vacuum as if it might nourish.

2/

reflect on the etymologies of husbandry and economy.
dream of fishes and loaves, though the shelves are emptied.

3/

sift through diaries of pandemic to assess the span of a life
lived too mildly. rehearse vigils and genuflections.

4/

ride the rollercoaster of conflicting graphs, swooping
the peaks and troughs of their projections.

5/

od on ocd, imagine the microscopic intimacies
as our cells are gate-crashed and compromised.

6/

feign surprise at the informality of goldfinches
pecking serenely at the rutted earth.

Insecticide

1/
2006

The mosquito's kettle wheeze
stirred me from
the deepest folds of dream.

Her heat-seeking night vision
seemed enabled
by my blood's glow,
and enhanced by maternal instinct:
to grow her young
or die trying.

I visualized her proboscis
as a pinprick,
from which disease could infiltrate.
And I feared it.

The next morning when
I confessed she'd breached the net,
you reproached me
for crushing her
into a sullen stain
on the unplastered wall.

You waxed allegorical, spoke in saws.
Stagnant waters are a breeding ground
for selfish hearts.
By lashing out at pain, we nourish
a million wars.

And I asked you if
a crash course in Karma
could neutralize our instinct
to avenge raw, punctured skin.

2/
2016

You are now a Bodhisattva.

And in ten years
the moral landscape
has been modified
as researchers
have delved new boundaries,

so I can now define two modes of *insecticide*:

1. DEET, like a clingfilm on the skin, to ward off bloodsuckers.
2. the culling of an entire species, *aedes aegypti*.

And their rigorous aim
would eradicate the virus
that can smite the brain
of a human foetus.

And with zealous intent
they alter the male,
so its offspring perish
like mayflies.

And I sympathize with your struggle
to extend compassion
to those who plot such extinction.

3/
2018

(i)

In muggy swamplands, skeeter swarms swelter.

In landfills, scourges breed in cracked cisterns.

Newborn humans perspire under netting,
their soft skin spared from lumpen sores.

Stranded truck drivers hunker down in darkness,
citronella coils wafting, histamines on high alert.

(ii)

But now science can splice
                pain from poison,
                        isolate bite from fever,

having identified a bacteria
                to inhibit zika.

And so to smoosh
a mosquito mother in mid-feed
may in time be seen
as an unenlightened reflex,

as if the burst blood
of my reluctant donation
crusts, itches, swells
like a stigmata.

Coalescence

'One's not half two. It's two are halves of one'
—e e cummings

There's a theory that our daughters' DNA
        has been shed within you.
And as my genes are wrapped up in
        their helices,
vestiges of me now flow in your blood,
        as if rust in your haemoglobin –
so our merger has surpassed
        the sum of our vows.

Dearest, whilst teaching that one and one
        don't always make two,

I realise you also bear the signature
        of our first miscarriage.
Its elegy of alleles still echoes
        within you, a reminder
of a coalescence that could
        not be sustained,
for we are two halves of the pain
        derived from this single rupture.

Haiki on the house

In the unkempt grass,
cinnabars lured by ragwort
feast on bursts of flame

Red admiral docked
on the drying white bedsheet –
inkblot, soon to blur

Rains revive the grass –
stars of borage and clover
ticklish underfoot

Formic fizz, last rites –
of a stray red ant, crumpled
though the swelling soothes

B&Q Buddha

It's said a marble Buddha
darkens/as it weathers/
and deposits of iron pyrites/
oxidise within/

So as moisture permeates/
and the ferrous residue
rusts/would it be too
far-fetched/to suggest

that this replica *respires*/

even as its breath seems/
forever clenched/
on the brink of release?

I can't justify the expense/
choose a polyresin clone instead.

The barcode bleeps/on this
generically squat/special offer/
hollow avatar/reproduced

on the treadmill/
of the unconscious machine.

3/

I absorb the glisten of
its factory fresh moulding,
as if
a just-cast bell cools in its cast.

4/

I parse its cryptic smile, pursed
as if
a pincered moth resists revelation.

5/

Imagine duplicate Buddha
sat in vigil
where the hedgerow
meets the pond/

the L-shape
of its straight back
and lotus tuck/

its eyelids like
dark petals/
flecked with lilyturf.

6/

Is this true meditation/then/
this solitude/in which

I feel orphaned/

until I anchor/
in the breath?

This book belongs to…
A & E, NHS

1/

The pushy drunk is hounding reception.

Shielded from exposure
to his blinding invective,
a nurse ushers us to an annexe
of the children's ward,
and cordons it off
like a panic room.

Fear is a fast contagion.

But sealed within,
they deem us immune,
as his f-words filter through
their threat of infection.

2/

Yet the longer we fester
in this sterile sanctum,
the more *our* crumpled states
seem fit for quarantine,

if merely to judge from
the gaunt mother
stealing shut eye
when her baby
doesn't splutter,

or the shell-shocked couple
who mutter, tracing

their evening back
to breaking point.

And we are no different:
anxious parents bound to protocol,
here as a precaution, still
flummoxed that fever could
make Amber convulse and jolt.

3/

Minutes grind by.
The toy box harbours mould,
so we home in on the crate of books.

With the flannel still damp on her brow,
we choose, from the tatty pile,
a Ladybird guide to *The Marine Life*.

'There are many creatures in the sea' I begin.

And whispering the rest, I feel submerged by
these sleepless fates, here in the depths of 3am.

She seems more herself, love.
Maybe call it a night?

Roused, then, from cabin fever,
I skim over the narrative
of the ocean's pageantry,

and make believe to Amber
that we're divers who must venture
through the maze of white walls
beyond this submarine's confines.

Prepped for all predators,
guarding her in my grasp,

I hurtle toward the exit,
with heat-seeking fists
and elbows like harpoons.

4/

And in my periphery I glimpse
this washed-up Kraken:
his stitched-up brow
and gauze-spun scalp;
and the burst capillaries
of his nasal flesh,

as he stirs himself one last time
to repel the policemen
in their luminous scales
of high-vis scotchlite.

And as his adrenaline wanes,
he shrinks in shame,
his ego a bruised fish,
hung by the hook
that pierces its lip.

His whole frame heaves,
as if the boy within has sunk.
And his handcuffs clunk
like an anchor wedged
to the blue plastic seat.

Bathing

was it mum or dad   who taught me
to wash between   the legs   soap hard
and let water   winking sunset   cling drip
drop   slow meniscus   from wrinkled balls

did I perhaps   on reflection   teach myself
to bathe   hurrying   frothy palms
over lines of sweat   the yin of fingers
gracing the yang   of skin taut on bone

how many years   self-serving   did I never
know this intimate matter   of being locked
into a lover   lush rush of river
biceps clamped   into armpits   how many times

does Time sieve   yours regretfully   never learning
perhaps closeness   that might come
incarnating   a water God   o two-toned Vishnu
all four arms   ready to sponge

Keyed

1/

How, as I drive through
this Kentish hamlet,
an official document –

stuck to the windscreen
of an abandoned car –
dredges up another:

the envelope tucked
under the wiper blades
of my second-hand Toyota,

which, parked in the only
free space on
the ex-council estate,

was just out of eyeshot from
the end of terrace
I'd bought in haste.

How it excavates drama
ten years untold, the mind
games of territory and legacy,

I the only brown face
to venture that far
down the cul-de-sac,

let alone invest
in the potential of
a family home.

How the envelope placed
on the pristine windscreen
could only seem a threat.

How, feeling too raw
to reveal the note's
fiercely inked heart,

I brewed a tea,
and drew the curtains,
sipping slowly, as I took in

the bold capped scrawl
exhorting me to
PARK ELSEWHERE.

How the request sought vindication
from potted local history, accords
FROM BEFORE YOUR TIME.

How the envelope seemed
like a dove's flattened wing,
snared in the machinery

that had macheted its body,
before it was cast off into
the grip of tarmac and rubber.

3/

How the white flag on the paned glass,
signed SINCERELY, BLANCHE,
seemed to impose my surrender.

How her carless-ness wasn't the point;
how there was no racial subtext,
addressed as it was

TO WHOM IT MAY CONCERN,
impartial in its anonymity.
How I tried compassion, imagined

my ominous black car
as a jarring apparition
after her sixty years in that house.

4/

How an anonymous neighbour left
a message of support
in the letterbox.

How, to Blanche's chagrin,
I continued to transgress,
unsure how best to explain that I'd rather

her incensed decrees than
the car being keyed
every night I parked out front,

by the neighbour opposite,
or so we supposed, who desired
all three spaces whenever

his daughters' kids came to visit.
How each new scratch – terse
and unequivocal – was a cruel shorthand

inducing waves of self-reproach,
the writing on the wall that our time
was up, our welcome outstayed.

fists

the consultant discounts   our thesis
that her sickness is viral
is reluctant to rule   out sepsis
warns *indecision could be fatal*

so under the infrared lamp
six trained hands   roughly palpate
the smooth beige egg of
our baby's fist   seeking to cannulate

the glowing tributary   of her metacarpal vein

so panicked here   in this sordid light
we're slaves to   antibiotic logic
that's apologetic   and despotic
as these blunt jabs   pointlessly   bruise her

doctors   please desist   clear the room
give us headspace   let your fists   soften back
into fingers   and thumbs

calcified about   the needle's glint
let the stubborn grip
of your protocol   loosen
ditto my knuckles   clenched in denial
as I grip the pen   that bleeds consent

Goodbye, Bargain Basement

For David on his 80th birthday

We shuffle down this cramped aisle,
pore over its warped shelves,
and thumb these paperbacks
arranged in their guesswork of genres.

There's nostalgia in these peeling walls,
witness to our casual quests,
as we've scoured second-hand philosophies,
or flirted with fictions hyped beyond us.

For old time's sake we try to divine
a reading order from the riddle
of these creased spines: *The Hours, Mrs Dalloway,
The Postpartum Husband, On Suicide.*

And I squat over the plastic crates,
seeking one more fable for Amber,
risking paper cuts as I rifle through
the misdeeds of cartoon pigs and cats.

Heavy with our last haul, we leave
mouthing farewells, and fast forward weeks
to see the whitened weft of cobwebs,
and the thick air yearning to be exorcised.

We will feel the lure of the bookstore in town,
its refurbished café and brand new floors,
happy that Amber can scamper like a zephyr
in its wide expanse. And you'll nurse a coffee,

sunk deep in a sofa, delving at leisure into
The Better Nature of Angels, while I'll slip away
to skim through the unread verse
in the basement of neglected bargains.

Nets

i.m. Jon Blackstaffe, 1977-2019

1/

No one else to vouch for us
that high noon in the rec.

Two late teens duelling it out
in early summer, stubborn in

our Sixth Form swagger –
my straggly goatee, curled at the fringes,

your mutton chops: copyright Led Zep,
via the Wild West.

You took guard in gloves, shorts and
one front pad; a replica Chelsea top,

but no helmet, only a Chicago Bears
baseball cap, so I vowed to aim low,

drying my sweaty palms
on the parched grass,

so no stray beamer
would slip from my grasp.

2/

The sun had baked the pitch dry,
a flat track yielding scant variation.

So I bent my back into it,
fizzing each ball in hard.

Over-pitched, the faded red orb
was dispatched with venom.

Four you boomed, or was it *fore?*

The merest hint of a crooked line,
pitching down leg, and you'd flick
the ball away with a flourish.

So I extended my run-up
to psyche you out,
but kept it short enough that

I didn't lose myself,
pelting in, feigning fury,
limber, elastic.

3/

In these months after your death,
I've tried to teleport back, to relive

the metallic whiff of sweat,
the trilling soundtrack of sparrows,

the slow trudge back to the coke can
that marked my start line,

the way I rehearsed
beating your outside edge,

bamboozling you with
a slower one, an impossible off-cutter.

4/

And I'm fixated, in truth,
by every dot ball –

the skill of attrition

each time my slingshot
scudded into your bat,
parried by soft hands
that snuffed out its bounce,

imagining now
how no single stalemate seemed futile,
how, between friends, there's no net gain.

5/

Let our loved ones picture us, then,
as patient adversaries, a brown
and a white boy, testosterone
harnessed by this ritual,

with success and failure,
pull stroke and maiden
all incidental to this drama,

of duels that bring no victor,

omitted by the scorecard,
perhaps, for being unspectacular.

ACKNOWLEDGEMENTS

Gratitude to the editors of the following publications, in which versions of some of these poems first appeared –

Ambit, Bad Lilies, bath magg, Magma, The North, Planet, Poetry Ireland Review, Poetry London, Poetry Wales, Rabbit (Australia) The Rialto, Stand.

'Seed' was longlisted for the Plough International Prize 2018, judged by Pascale Petit.

'Goodbye, Bargain Basement' appears in 'Off The Shelf' (2016, Picador) edited by Carol Ann Duffy.

Thanks to Sarah Westcott and Sophia Bartleet for close reading, feedback and advice.

Immense gratitude to my daughter, Amber (aged 10), for the cover image. Many thanks to both Charley Openshaw and Fran Hodgson for helping to curate its final look.

An enormous debt to Rob for giving this collection a home, and for his patience and rigour.

Neetha Kunaratnam was awarded the Geoffrey Dearmer Prize for 2007. He gained an MA in Creative Writing in 2008 from Royal Holloway, studying under Andrew Motion and Jo Shapcott.

His work appears in the anthologies *Off the Shelf,* (Picador, 2016) and *Out of Sri Lanka* (Bloodaxe, 2023)

His first collection *Just Because* (Smokestack Books) was highly commended in the 2019 Forward Prizes and he features in The Forward Prizes Poems of the Decade 2011-20.

He is a teacher and lives in East Sussex with his wife and two daughters.